THEMATIC UNIT

SEA ANIMALS

Written by Diane Williams

Edited by Patricia Miriani
Illustrated by Keith Vasconcelles

Teacher Created Materials, Inc.
P.O. Box 1040
Huntington Beach, CA 92647
©1993 Teacher Created Materials, Inc.
Made in U.S.A.

ISBN 1-55734-254-7

Table of Contents

Introduction

Sea Animals contains a captivating whole language thematic unit. Its 80 exciting pages are filled with a wide variety of lesson ideas and activities designed for use with children at the early childhood level. For each of the two featured books, activities are included which set the stage for reading, encourage the enjoyment of the book, and extend the concepts gained. In addition, the theme is connected to the curriculum with activities in language arts (including language experience and writing suggestions), math, science, art, music, and life skills (cooking, physical education, etc.). Many of these activities encourage cooperative learning. Suggestions and patterns for bulletin boards are additional time savers for the busy teacher. Furthermore, directions for student-created Big Books and culminating activities, which allow students to synthesize their knowledge in order to produce products that can be shared beyond the classroom, highlight this very complete teacher resource.

This thematic unit includes:

❏ **Literature selections**—summaries of two children's books with related lessons (complete with reproducible pages) that cross the curriculum

❏ **Language experience and writing ideas**—suggestions as well as activities across the curriculum, including Big Books

❏ **Bulletin board ideas**—suggestions and plans for student-created and/or interactive bulletin boards

❏ **Homework suggestions**—extending the unit to the child's home

❏ **Curriculum connections**—in language arts, math, science, art, music, and life skills such as cooking, and physical education

❏ **Group projects**—to foster cooperative learning

❏ **Culminating activities**—which require students to synthesize their learning to produce a product or engage in an activity that can be shared with others

❏ **A bibliography**—suggesting additional literature and nonfiction books on the theme

> To keep this valuable resource intact so it can be used year after year, you may wish to punch holes in the pages and store them in a three-ring binder.

Introduction (cont.)

Why Whole Language?

A whole language approach involves children in using all modes of communication: reading, writing, listening, observing, illustrating, experiencing, and doing. Communication skills are interconnected and integrated into lessons that emphasize the whole of language rather than isolating its parts. The lessons revolve around selected literature. Reading is not taught as a separate subject from writing and spelling, for example. A child reads, writes (spelling appropriately for his/her level), speaks, listens, etc., in response to a literature experience introduced by the teacher. In this way, language skills grow naturally, stimulated by involvement and interest in the topic at hand.

Why Thematic Planning?

One very useful tool for implementing an integrated whole language program is thematic planning. By choosing a theme with correlating literature selections for a unit of study, a teacher can plan activities throughout the day that lead to a cohesive, in-depth study of the topic. Students will be practicing and applying their skills in meaningful contexts. Consequently, they will tend to learn and retain more. Both teachers and students will be freed from a day that is broken into unrelated segments of isolated drill and practice.

Why Cooperative Learning?

Besides academic skills and content, students need to learn social skills. No longer can this area of development be taken for granted. Students must learn to work cooperatively in groups in order to function well in modern society. Group activities should be a regular part of school life, and teachers should consciously include social objectives as well as academic objectives in their planning. For example, a group working together to solve a problem may need to select a leader. The teacher should make clear to the students and monitor the qualities of good leader-follower group interaction just as he/she would state and monitor the academic goals of the project.

Why Big Books?

An excellent cooperative, whole language activity is the production of Big Books. Groups of students, or the whole class, can apply their language skills, content knowledge, and creativity to produce a Big Book that can become a part of the classroom library to be read and reread. These books make excellent culminating projects for sharing beyond the classroom with parents, librarians, other classes, etc. Big Books can be produced in many ways, and this thematic unit book includes directions for at least one method you may choose.

The Whales' Song

by Dyan Sheldon

Summary

The Whales' Song *is a very special book. It is a poignant story that touches your heart and soul. Lilly's grandmother shares a magical tale with her granddaughter. Long ago, when she was a child, she gave a special gift to the whales, and they in turn gave her a special gift of their own. Great-uncle Frederick stomps about, trying to snuff out the magic.*

Lilly longs to meet the whales. She dreams of them, believes in them, brings a gift, and then waits for them to find her. And they do.

The outline below is a suggested plan for using the various activities that are presented in this unit. You should adapt these ideas to fit your own classroom situation.

Sample Plan

Day 1

- Introduce activity centers. (page 6)
- Discuss ways to play at the sea.
- Make and illustrate a Big Book of "Play at the Sea."
- Read *The Whales' Song.*
- Review the story in depth.
- Art: Draw a favorite part of the story. (page 9)
- Make puppets. (page 11)
- Act out the story with puppets.

Day 2

- Activity Centers. (page 6)
- Review the Big Book. (Play lists)
- P.E.: - Creative Movement. (page 8)
- Reread the story.
- Act out the story.

- Math: "A Whale Is Taller Than I Am" (page 22); send home page 23.
- Art: "Sea Sillies." (page 25)

Day 3

- Activity Centers. (page 6)
- Review the story by sharing puppet plays and creative drama.
- Math: "A Whale Is Heavier Than I Am." (page 22)
- Share a nonfiction book about humpbacks.
- Discuss and compare your body and the body of a humpback whale.
- Do "My Body" and "A Whale's Body." (pages 20-21)
- Music: Learn "Baby Beluga." (page 8)
- Art: Finger Painting. (page 25)

Overview of Activities

SETTING THE STAGE

1. Have the children pretend they are spending a day at the beach. Fill a sandbox with sand. Collect the following things and put them in a box:

   beach bags

   beach towels

   sand pails

   sand shovels

   collection of shells and pebbles

   toy boats

   empty bottle of suntan oil

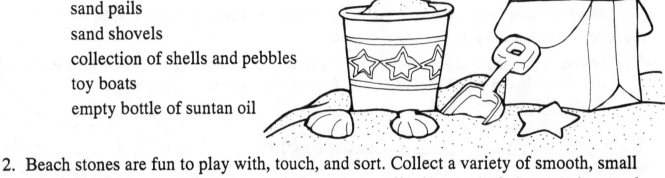

2. Beach stones are fun to play with, touch, and sort. Collect a variety of smooth, small beach pebbles and put them in a pail. Set out a small tub or pan of water, and a towel on a table. Have students play counting games, make designs with stones, and sort according to size or color.

3. Set out a display of books and pictures of whales in the class library. See bibliography on page 79 for suggested titles.

4. Set out a collection of water music. (See bibliography.) Include Raffi's "Baby Beluga" record or tape and "Songs of the Humpback Whale" record (see bibliography).

5. Discuss ways to "Play Beside the Sea," "Play On Top of the Sea," and "Play Under the Sea." Make a cooperative list for each on chart paper. Ask the children to draw a picture to go with one idea on the chart. Use the ideas from the charts to create a Big Book. You may make three separate books, one for each category.

6. Suggest that the children bring photographs from home of their holidays by the water and tell about them. Which ones were their favorites? Which seas did they visit? Set out a pile of old magazines. Ask the children to find pictures of people playing by/on/ under the sea. Have the children cut out the pictures and paste them into a scrapbook or into the Big Book.

Overview of Activities (cont.)

ENJOYING THE STORY

1. Read *The Whales' Song* for enjoyment. Set the stage for a special sharing time. Have the children sit on the carpet close to you. Ensure there will be no interruptions. Read it slowly, savoring the poetic text, giving lots of time to appreciate each painting. Let the magic of the story surround you.

2. Review the story, asking some of the following questions:
   - Why are whales special?
   - Why did the whales swim to Grandma?
   - What special gift did the whales give to Grandma?
   - What does Great-uncle Frederick say about whales?
   - What would you have said to him?
   - Why did Lilly drop a flower into the ocean the next day?
   - What woke Lilly up that special night?
   - What did the whales give Lilly?
   - Do you think Lilly was dreaming?
   - Do you think the whales really called her name?

3. This story is rich with important questions. Use it to stimulate critical thinking but be sure to set a tone of trust, accepting all feelings and ideas. Use the quotes from the story and ask questions.

   "People used to say they were magical."
   Ask the children to express how they feel about the whales.
   Do you think the whales were magical? Why or why not?
   "People used to eat them and boil them down for oil!"
   How do you feel about this? Why?
   "Enough of this foolishness...Come on home.
   You can't be dreaming your life away."
   Do you think Lilly is dreaming her life away? Why or why not?
   Why do you think Great-uncle Frederick said that?

4. Have students draw and color pictures of their favorite parts of the story (page 9).

5. Examine the theme. Control the tone so the children can safely discuss their feelings and beliefs without ridicule or criticism. Set the tone by sharing something magical that happened to you. By sharing one of your personal magical moments, you show the children it is all right to cherish a teddy, or wish on a star, or....

Overview of Activities *(cont.)*

EXTENDING THE STORY
---

1. Act out the story. Allow the children to ad lib. Use simple costumes such as a nightie for Lilly, a wig or old dress for Grandma, and a big old cardigan for Great-uncle Frederick. Spread an old blue blanket on the rug for a makeshift ocean. Challenge some of the children to move like whales in the ocean.

2. Make finger puppets (see page 11). Have fun acting out the story with a friend or two.

3. Do any art activities suggested on pages 25-26: Finger Painting, Sand Drawing, Sea Sillies, Magic Drawing, Stuff a Sea Creature, or Hang Up the Sea.

4. Learn the song "Baby Beluga" by Raffi. (See bibliography.) Listen to a recording of the Humpback Whales' songs. (See bibliography.) Learn "Under the Sea" from *The Little Mermaid* by Walt Disney.

5. Challenge the children to become whales! Play the recording of the Humpback Whales' songs in the background. Let them use "flippers" to swim or dive down to the bottom of the ocean.

6. Find out how far the whales migrate each year. Mark it on a large map or globe. Compare the family life of whales to yours.

7. Discuss how a whale is like you and not like you. Color a whale's body, then your own body. Compare.

8. Do some reading for information. Make a Big Book using pages 13-17. Have students make the accompanying little book (pages 18-19). Let them color, cut out, and assemble the little book. They may wish to make a cover with the title, "My Little Book About Whales" or use the one provided on page 13.

9. "A Whale Is Huge!" activities (page 22) involve estimation and measurement activities on page 22. Pages 23-24 are for students to take home to be filled out by their parents.

10. Read *The Story of Three Whales* for fun. (See bibliography.) Read *Why The Sun And The Moon Live In The Sky*. (See bibliography.) It is a wonderful African folktale which would be fun to use for creative drama.

Name_____

My Favorite Part

Draw a picture of your favorite part of the story.

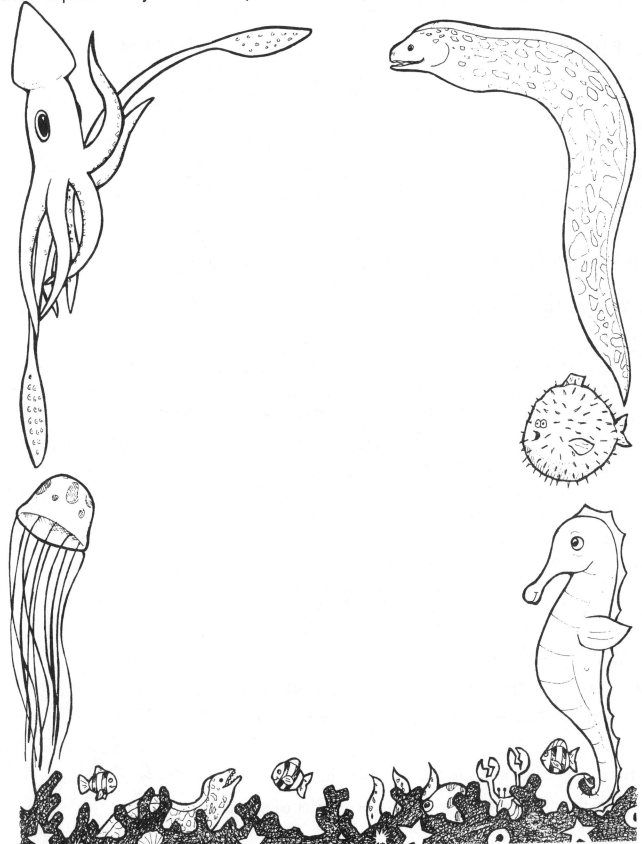

Creative Drama Activities

Creative drama is a land of magic for children. It develops creativity, language, self-expression, and communication skills.

Make Puppets

Finger Puppets: Have children color and cut out the patterns on page 11. Paste the bottom into a circle to fit the children's fingers.

Stick Puppets: Use any of the patterns on pages 71-75. The children can also draw their own real or imaginary sea animals with marking pens on heavy paper. These can be cut out and taped or stapled to a wide craft stick.

Make a Puppet Stage

Table: Hang an old sheet over a low table. The puppeteers simply kneel on the floor behind the table. The puppets move on top of the table.

Box: Cut a large square hole in the top half of a big box. Prop up the box securely. The puppeteers sit or kneel behind the box. The puppets move in the square hole.

Sheet: Hang a rope or heavy string across a corner of the room about 2 feet (60 cm) from the floor. Drop a sheet over the rope. The puppeteers kneel behind the sheet in the corner. The puppets move above the sheet.

Establish Rules

Have a class discussion to decide the rules for puppet play. Include a discussion about how to handle the puppets. Print the rules on a chart and display it in a creative drama center.

Make Puppet Plays

Choose one of the following ways to use the puppets and stages:

1. Let children play with the puppets by themselves. Use two puppets.

2. Have children choose a partner and make up plays for fun.

3. In small groups have children plan a play, practice it, and share it with others.

Finger Puppets

See page 10 for directions.

Something Magical!

Grandmother told Lilly that people used to say that whales were magical. It would be magical if you could make a whale out of a piece of paper. Follow the directions below to make a magical whale.

1. Cut out diamond. Fold along dotted lines.

2. Fold in half.

3. Fold tail. Cut the tail a little.

4. Draw a whale face on the whale.

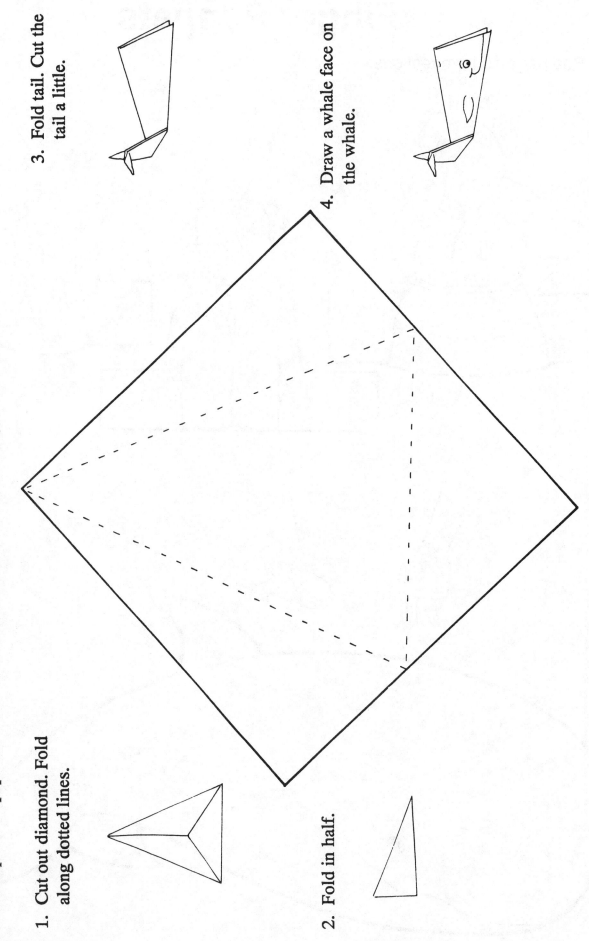

12

A Whale of a Book!

(See page 8, #8 for directions.)

The Humpback Whale

The humpback whale loves to swim. He swims from the Arctic Ocean to the Antarctic Ocean every year! And he loves to play. He waves, slaps his fins, and leaps up out of the water. The humpback whale is very special. He is a singing whale! No one knows why he sings. But he really does. He sings beautiful songs day and night.

The Blue Whale

The blue whale is the biggest animal on earth. He is even bigger than the biggest dinosaur! Even a baby blue whale is huge. He is 23 feet (7 m) long when he is born! He eats 300 pounds (136 kg) of his mother's milk a day! The blue whale is huge but harmless. This biggest animal on earth eats tiny creatures in the sea!

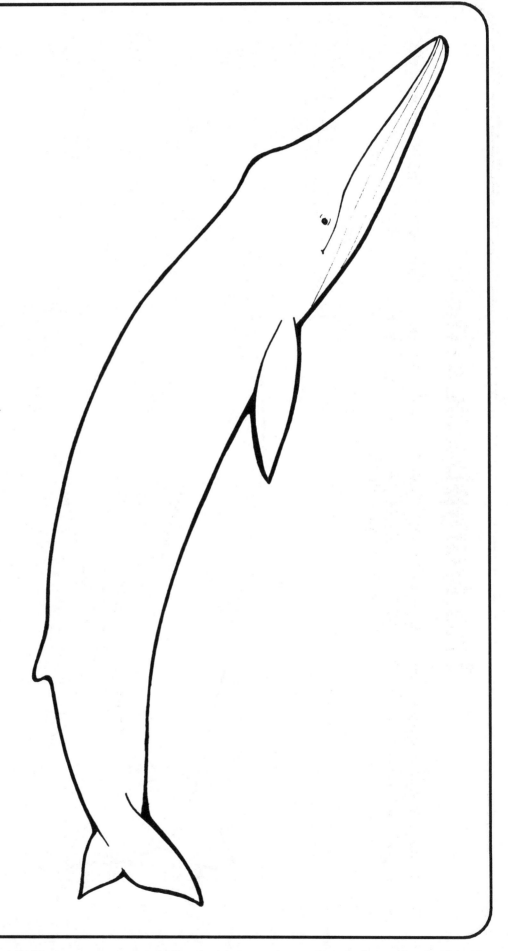

The Beluga Whale

"Beluga" means "white whale" in Russian. He lives in the Arctic Ocean. His fat keeps him warm. The beluga whale is playful and noisy. When he is in an aquarium, he likes to squirt people with water!

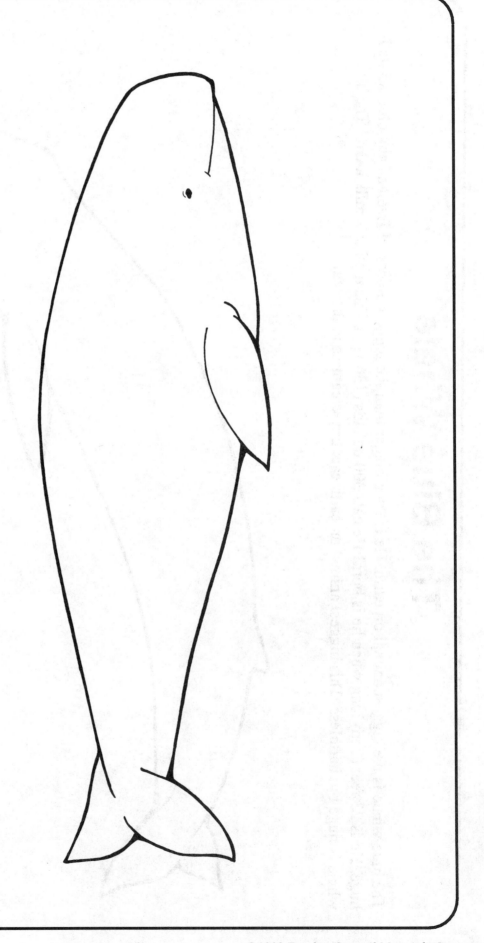

Killer Whales

These animals should not be called killer whales. They do not kill us. Killer whales are also called "orcas." Killer whales are very big. They eat seals, sea lions, penguins, and fish. Killer whales are very smart. They can talk to each other by using their blow holes. Scientists think they have different languages just like us!

Little Book

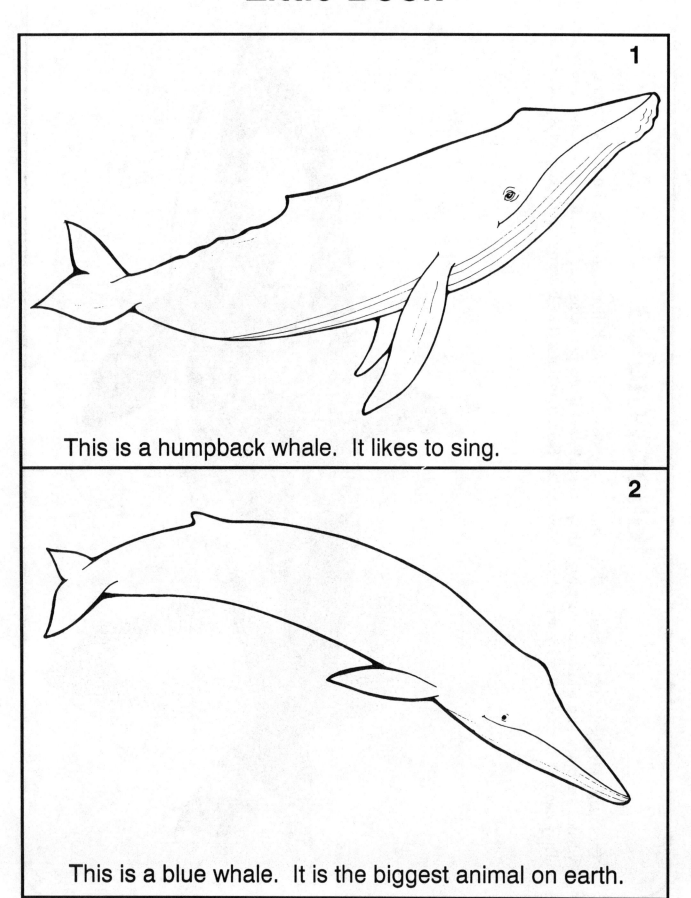

1

This is a humpback whale. It likes to sing.

2

This is a blue whale. It is the biggest animal on earth.

Little Book *(cont.)*

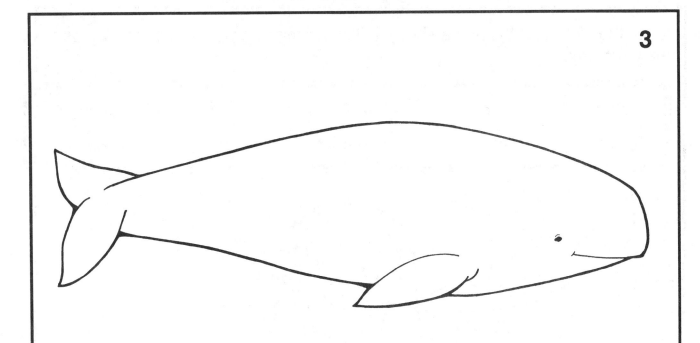

3

This is a beluga whale. *Beluga* means "white whale" in Russian.

4

This is a killer whale. Its real name is *orca*.

Name _____

My Body

Color the picture of the human body. Fill in the missing words. Use the words from the word box.

head	leg	hand	eye	mouth
arm	foot	stomach	ear	nose

Name_____

A Whale's Body

Color the picture of a whale's body. Fill in the missing words. Use the words from the word box.

blow hole	stomach	head
eye	tail	flipper

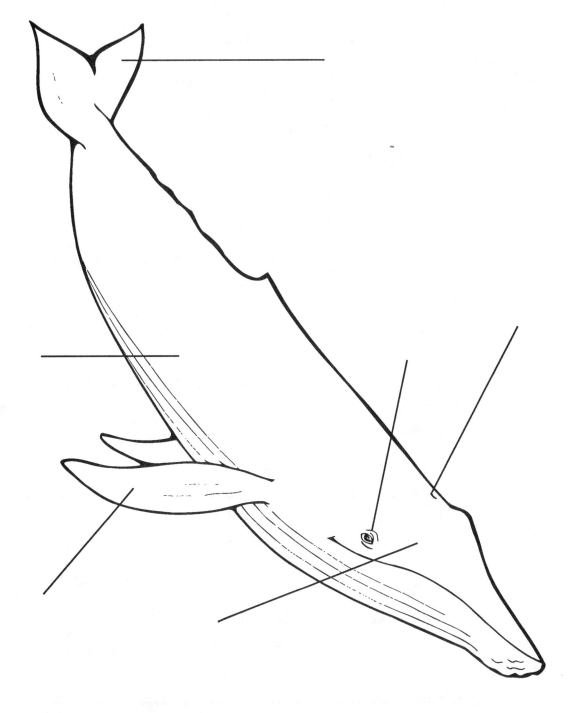

A Whale Is Huge!

How big is a whale? How much does it eat? Let children complete these activities to find out.

A Whale Is Taller Than I Am

- Discuss how big whales are compared to other creatures.
- Discuss ways to measure whales. Measure the distance from one child's outstretched hand to the other. Estimate how many of these units would equal the length of one humpback and stand hand to hand to show this.
- Work out the average height of all the children. Estimate how many of these units would equal the height of one humpback. Lie down head to toe on a grassy field to show how tall a humpback is.
- Have students take home "A Whale Is Taller Than I Am" (page 23) to be completed with their parents.

A Whale Is Heavier Than I Am

- Discuss how heavy whales are compared to other creatures and how heavy a child is compared to other creatures.
- Use a scale to weigh each child. Work out an average weight. Estimate how many of these units would equal the weight of one humpback. Have that many children stand all together to demonstrate the weight.

A Whale Is Hungrier Than I Am

- Discuss the foods a humpback eats. Compare this to what children eat.
- Ask children to keep a record of what they eat in one day. Have them draw and color pictures of all the food they eat in one day.
- Find out what a humpback eats in one day and draw pictures of all the food he eats in one day.
- Find out what a baby humpback eats in one day.
- Have students take home "A Whale Is Hungrier Than I Am" (page 24) to be completed with their parents.

22

Name_____

A Whale Is Huge! *(cont.)*

A whale is taller than I am

1. When he is born, a baby humpback whale is as long as a station wagon!

   When I was born, I was as long as _____ .

2. A grown-up humpback whale is longer than a big bus!

   When I am a grown-up, I will be taller than a _____ .

3. Guess how long a humpback whale is. _____ .

   Measure how tall you are. _____ .

4. Draw a picture of yourself standing beside the whale.

A Whale Is Huge!

A whale is hungrier than I am

1. A baby whale can drink about 100 gallons (84 imperial gallons) of milk in one day!

   When I was a baby, I drank about _____ gallons of milk in one day.

2. A baby whale gains about 200 pounds (90 kg) in ONE day!

   When I was a baby, I gained about _____ pounds (grams) in one day.

3. If you were bottle feeding a baby whale, how big do you think his bottle would be?

   Draw a picture of the baby whale bottle.

Art Activities

Finger Painting

Materials: 1 part water; 1 part flour; heavy paper; blue, green, and turquoise powder paints; aprons; paper; felt pens; bowls; scissors; spoons; paste

Preparation: Make the homemade paste by mixing the water and flour together, stirring constantly. Divide the paste into several bowls. Add a different color of powder paint to each bowl. Put on some "ocean music" and let the children slip and slide through their oceans.

Directions: Dampen the table top so the paper will not slip. Put some finger paint onto the paper, and let children slide their fingers through it. Let this ocean background dry. On a separate sheet of paper, have children draw and color whales with felt pens. Have them cut these out and paste them onto the dried ocean background to make an ocean scene.

Sand Drawing

Materials: sand; squeeze paste bottles; newspapers; pieces of cardboard

Directions: Spread newspaper over the table. Let children draw a sea picture by squeezing the paste onto the cardboard and sprinkling sand onto it. Let it dry. Tip the loose sand off onto the newspaper.

Sea Sillies

Materials: paper; thin black marker; colored construction paper; paste; scissors

Directions: Have children make a tracing of one of their hands onto the paper using a thin black marker. Make the hand tracing into a Sea Silly by coloring it. Have children make a sea picture by coloring the background. Ask them to write a silly story about their Sea Sillies.

Art Activities *(cont.)*

Stuff a Sea Creature

Materials: tempera paints; large sheets of paper; brushes; scissors; felt pens; stapler; newspapers; tape

Directions: Have children draw a huge sea creature with felt pens. Let them place another sheet of paper behind it and cut out two (or cut one, trace it, and cut the other separately). Paint both outsides of the sea creature. Let it dry. Staple the two pieces together, leaving an opening on one side. Stuff your creature with scrunched newspapers. Staple shut.

Hang Up the Sea!

Materials: green, turquoise, and blue crepe paper; string; tape; stuffed sea creatures

Directions: Hang long pieces of string from one side of the classroom to the other, along the ceiling. Tape a piece of string onto the stuffed sea creatures (see above) and hang them up. Cut the blue and turquoise crepe paper into long strips. Tape or tie one end to one side of the classroom ceiling. Twist the crepe paper gently to make "waves" or "currents." Tape or tie the other end of the crepe paper to the other side of the ceiling. Cut the green crepe paper into shorter strips of various widths or shapes. Hang these down from the ceiling strings to make "seaweed" and "plants." Twist pieces of crepe paper into shapes like sea plants. Tape onto the counter. Tape blue cellophane onto the windows, or put a blue light bulb in a lamp.

26

Animals of Sea and Shore

by Illa Podendorf

Summary

Animals of Sea and Shore *is a wonderful nonfiction book for young children. It is rich in information, well organized, and useful for teaching early research skills.*

The ocean is filled with a myriad of life forms—far too many to study. This book organizes ocean animal life into six simple groups and describes each group, giving interesting examples of each.

The outline below is a suggested plan for using the various activities that are presented in this unit. You should adapt these ideas to fit your own classroom situation.

Sample Plan

Day 1

- Activity Centers. (page 28)
- Read "Animals With Fur."
- Group Discussion. (page 29)
- Play "Sea Things" game. (page 31)
- Play "Going Fishing." (pages 50, 51)
- Music: Learn "Rubber Blubber Whale," and sing "Baby Beluga."
- Art: Fun On A Stick. (page 57)

Day 2

- Activity Centers. (page 28)
- Fish Skeleton. (page 32, #10)
- P.E.: Be a Whale, Seal
- Read "Animals With Fins."
- Group Discussion. (page 29)
- Do a Seawater Experiment. (page 54)
- Set up class aquarium. (page 28)
- Play "Sea Animal Concentration." (pages 36-37)
- Art: Make "Fish Prints." (page 57)

- Music: Sing "Rubber Blubber Whale" "Three Little Fishies."

Day 3

- Activity Centers. (page 28)
- Read "Animals With Many Legs."
- Group Discussion. (page 29.)
- Draw a story. (page 47)
- Math: Connect the Dots; "Going Fishing." (pages 49, 50, 51)
- Creative Drama: Act out the story.
- Music: Learn "Way Down Here Beneath the Ocean" and "Three Little Fishies."
- Make shell collages. (page 58)

Day 4

- Activity Centers. (page 28)
- Read the rest of the book beginning with "Animals with Shells." Discuss. (page 30)
- Play Octopus. (page 68)
- Try a seafaring recipe. (pages 66-67)
- Begin a Culminating Activity. (pages 69-70)

Overview of Activities

SETTING THE STAGE

1. Make a class "touching pond" using an old baby bathtub or water box. Put some sand, rocks, and pebbles in the bottom. Fill half full with cold water. Add a few shells such as clams and scallops from the seafood section of the market, shells from the beach, and/or one or two special shells from the pet or shell store. Go to the seafood section of the market and get a few prawns in the shell, small squid, kippers, a small whole fish, sardines, etc. Put two of each in the freezer and one in the touching pond. Add ice to the pond. At the end of the day, throw it away. The next day, put out new ones from the freezer.

2. Buy brine shrimp, also known as sea monkeys, from a pet store, complete with jar, food, and instructions. Set out magnifying glasses, and a simplified version of the instructions. Ask the class to help you set up the sea monkeys' home. Delegate the care of the sea monkeys to the children. Encourage the children to observe developments daily.

3. Set up a class aquarium—borrow things from another class or family or go on a field trip to the pet store. An inexpensive, easy aquarium is simply a goldfish in a bowl. Set out some books about the care of fish. Make a class list of rules: "How To Care For Fish."

4. Make a list of fish names from A to Z. Fill an aquarium with donations of fish. Prepare ABC name cards and display.

5. Set out a wonderful display of books and photographs of sea life in the class library. Put out an air mattress and blue blankets or beach towels to float on while reading.

6. Set out a collection of "water music." (See bibliography.) Offer a record player or tape recorder as necessary.

7. Borrow a shell collection and put it on display. Add a book or two about shells. Challenge the children to identify the various shells and shell families.

8. Watch a filmstrip about sea life. (See bibliography.)

Overview of Activities *(cont.)*

ENJOYING THE STORY

Animals of Sea and Shore is a nonfiction book rich in information. It is best presented one part at a time. The children can record their research by making a Big Book a little at a time. Print the title of the book on a piece of chart paper. This will be page 1 of the Big Book.

1. Read "Animals With Fur." Ask the children to swim back to the storytime carpet, then to climb out of the water and sit on the rocks and sand. Then read for enjoyment. List the title of part one on Big Book page 1.

   Group Discussion:
   • What are animals with fur like?
   • How are they like us?
   • How are they different from us?

   Group Composition:
   • Print "Animals With Fur" on Big Book page 2.
   • Ask the children to tell about animals with fur in their own words.
   • Illustrate the group composition.

2. Read "Animals With Fins." Ask the children to put on a snorkel and mask and jump into the ocean! Read for enjoyment. List the title of part two on Big Book page 1.

   Group Discussion:
   • What are animals with fins like?
   • How are they like us?
   • How are they different from us?

   Group Composition:
   • Print "Animals With Fins" on Big Book page 3.
   • Ask the children to tell about animals with fins.
   • Illustrate the group composition.

   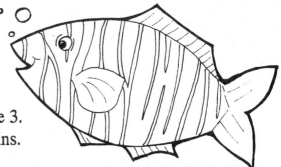

3. Read "Animals With Many Legs." Ask the children to get into scuba gear and get ready to dive deep into the ocean! Read for enjoyment. List the title of part three on Big Book page 1.

   Group Discussion:
   • What are animals with many legs like?
   • How are they like us?
   • How are they different from us?

   Group Composition
   • Print "Animals With Many Legs" on Big Book page 4.
   • Ask the children to tell about these in their own words.
   • Illustrate the group composition.

Overview of Activities *(cont.)*

ENJOYING THE STORY *(cont.)*

4. Read "Animals With Shells." Ask the children to swim out of the sea and explore on the shore. Read for enjoyment. List the title of part four on Big Book page 1.

   Group Discussion:
   • What are animals with shells like?
   • How are they like us?
   • How are they different from us?

   Group Composition:
   • Print "Animals With Shells" on Big Book page 5.
   • Ask the children to tell about these in their own words.
   • Illustrate the group composition.

5. Read "Animals With Spiny Skins." Ask the children to explore tidal pools and shallow water with you. Read for enjoyment. List the title of part five on Big Book page 1.

   Group Discussion:
   • What are animals with spiny skins like?
   • How are they like us?
   • How are they different from us?

   Group Composition:
   • Print "Animals With Spiny Skins" on Big Book page 6.
   • Ask the children to tell about these in their own words.
   • Illustrate the group composition.

6. Read "Animals With Soft Bodies." Ask the children to put on their suits and snorkels and go swimming! Read for enjoyment.

   Group Discussion:
   • What are animals with soft bodies like?
   • How are they like us?
   • How are they different from us?

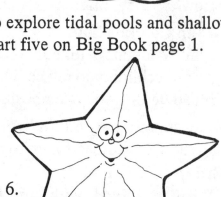

   Group Composition:
   • Print "Animals With Soft Bodies" on Big Book page 7.
   • Ask the children to tell about these in their own words.
   • Illustrate the group composition.

   Note: Activities 1-6 on pages 29 and 30 lend themselves to using a Venn diagram.

7. Read "Things To Remember." Read for enjoyment. Review the pages of the Big Book together. Make a title page. Staple it all together into book form. Share it with another class at their storytime or share it at Open House.

Overview of Activities *(cont.)*

EXTENDING THE STORY

1. Read "Believe It Or Not!" facts (page 38). Play "Fishy Games" to develop listening, oral, and spelling skills (page 41).

2. Put a variety of sea things on a tray. Cover it with a tea towel or cloth. Show the tray to a small group of children for 30 seconds. Cover it up. Ask them to tell what they saw on the tray. Show the tray to a small group of children for 30 seconds. Cover it up and secretly remove one item. Show the tray again and ask, "Which item is missing?" Suggest they play these games with each other in their free time.

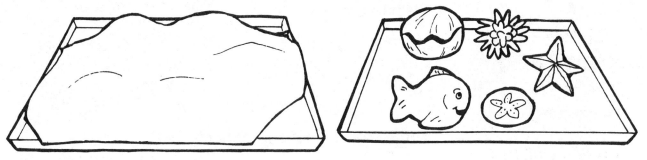

3. Complete "Would you rather be...." (page 44). Discuss and debate. Do activity pages and then share. Have fun!

4. Cut out pictures of fish from magazines or use pattern pages 71-75 and laminate each picture. Cut into simple puzzle pieces. Wash out a tuna or salmon can and tape the edge with masking tape for safety. Put each puzzle in a tin.

5. Cut out pictures of 5 different fish. (See pages 71-75.) Paste a piece of different colored construction paper to the back of each. Laminate each picture. Cut into simple puzzle pieces. Put all the pieces into one shoe box. Challenge the children to do all 5 puzzles at once, and identify what they are.

6. Challenge the children to turn on their imaginations! Have them draw a strange sea creature and dictate a story about the creature. Share the stories with the class.

Overview of Activities *(cont.)*

EXTENDING THE STORY *(cont.)*

7. As an introduction to the activity on page 39, read the following poem. Find the rhyming words and the rhythm. Have the children complete the activity on page 45.

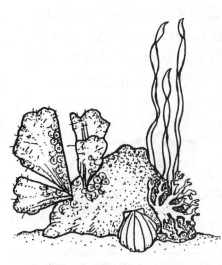

Dave the Octopus

I met an octopus under the sea,

I looked at him, he looked at me.

He sat in a cave,

His name was Dave.

I tried to say "Hi,"

But he was rather shy.

He zoomed away in a blur of pink,

And I was left in a sea of black ink!

by Bryn Williams - age 13

8. Children will enjoy the Draw a Story activity (page 47). Illustrate it as you tell it, letting them guess what the Sea Thing might be.

9. Do some math activities starting with the Dot-to-Dot Puzzle (page 49). Play with shells, sort, classify, count, and make patterns. Make a graph, "Can You Swim?" to show how many can and cannot swim. Discuss. Make a graph, "Did You Eat Sea Food Today?" Discuss. Count how many teeth each child has. Make a Graph. Compare to a shark.

10. Carefully remove the skeleton from a fish. Gently rinse it off, and put it on a piece of black construction paper on a platter. Set out a magnifying glass and a book showing the parts of a fish. Add a picture or model of the human skeleton if you can for comparison. Set up a Touching Pond, Class Aquarium, Microscope, and Sea Monkeys. Study how a fish breathes by watching the fish in the class aquarium. Study how a person breathes by watching a friend. Compare. "Do Fun With Sea Shells" activities (page 52).

11. Sharks have rows and rows of teeth, but we certainly do not. Display a photograph of the inside of a shark's mouth and the inside of a human's mouth. Ask the children to compare and evaluate. Ask them to draw pictures to show ways they can protect their teeth.

Overview of Activities *(cont.)*

EXTENDING THE STORY *(cont.)*

12. Read a book about safety. Talk about why rules are necessary. Make a cooperative group list of "Water Safety Rules" on a chart.

13. Read lots of the special books. Many are listed in the bibliography on pages 79-80. Let children bring in books about sea animals from home.

14. Let the children sing silly sea songs (page 55). Learn "Oh, I Went Into the Water" and "There's a Hole in the Bottom of the Sea" found in *The Silly Song Book*. Listen to "La Mer" while doing art projects. For fun, read *Clams Can't Sing* by James Stevenson. (See bibliography.) Try making sea sounds!

15. Read *Is This a House For Hermit Crab?* by Megan McDonald. Try spontaneous choral speaking. Suggest the children act out the story—let them invent the dialogue. Acting parts can include shell, rock, tin can, driftwood, plastic pail, hole in sand, fishing net, wave, pricklepine fish, empty shell, and hermit crab.

16. This unit offers a wealth of art activities. These include puppetry, printing, collage, mobiles, water jars, wax crayon melts, murals, stained glass fish, various painting skills, cut and paste projects, and drawing. Try some of them beginning on page 57.

17. Make a list of all the foods we eat from the ocean. Ask students to identify the animal from which the food came. Try some of the cooking activities on pages 64-67.

18. If you live close enough visit the ocean. Discuss how to treat the sea animals with respect. It is all right to touch, but remember the animal is afraid of humans so be gentle and then put it back where you found it. Take boots, pails, magnifying glasses, and a camera. Explore the shore and the tidal pools.

19. Take some trips. Go to an aquarium. Be sure to do some artwork as soon as you return. Go to a pet store. Study all the sea life, select fish for the class aquarium, and interview the staff about the care of fish. Go to a fish market. Learn about the sea animals we eat. Bring some back to school for the touching pond and a feast!

Feed the Sea Creature

Feed the fish with Ff words. Find Ff words in books and charts. Print them in the fish.

Name

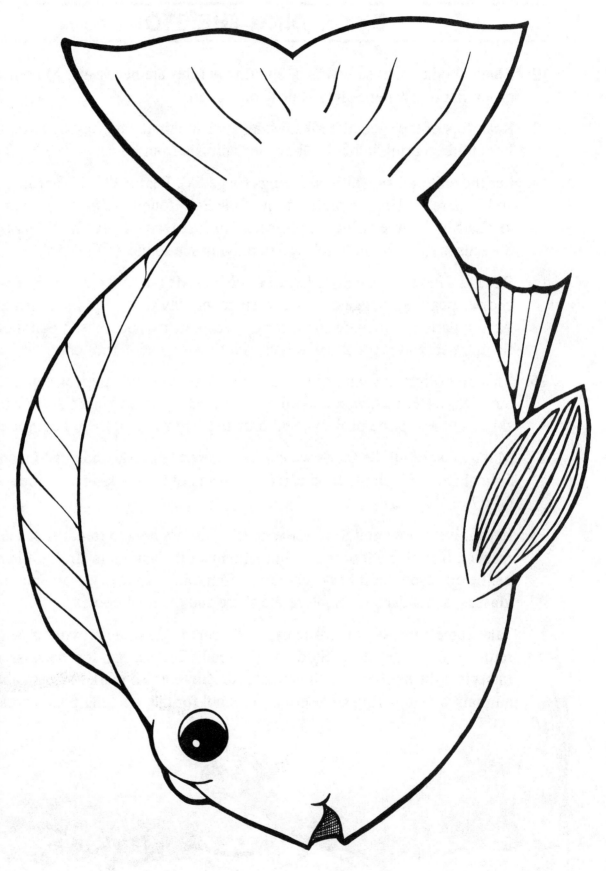

Name _____

Feed the Sea Creature *(cont.)*

Feed the starfish with Ss words. Find Ss words in books and charts. Print them in the starfish.

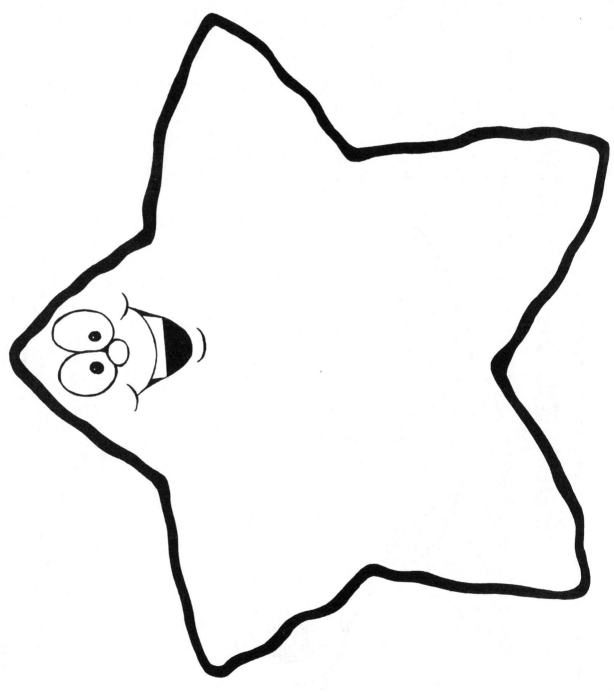

Sea Animal Concentration

Preparation:

• Make two copies each and cut out the cards below and on page 37. If additional cards are desired, the pictures on pages 42 and 43 may be used. You may wish to copy them onto tag board and/or laminate them for added durability. Color the cards if desired. Store the game cards in an envelope with game directions glued to the front.

Directions:

• The game is for 2-4 players. Mix up cards and lay them face down on a table. A player picks two cards. If the cards match, the player keeps the cards and takes another turn. If the two cards do not form a match, they are returned to their places face down on the table, and another player takes a turn. The game continues until all matches have been made. The player with the most matches is the winner.

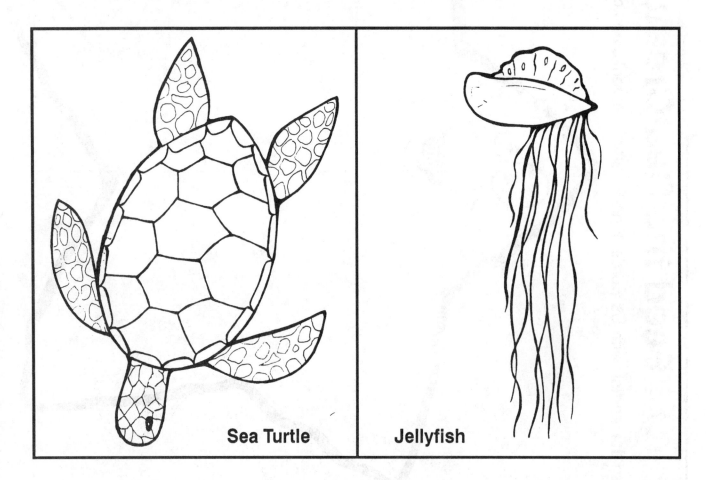

Sea Turtle　　　**Jellyfish**

Sea Animal Concentration *(cont.)*

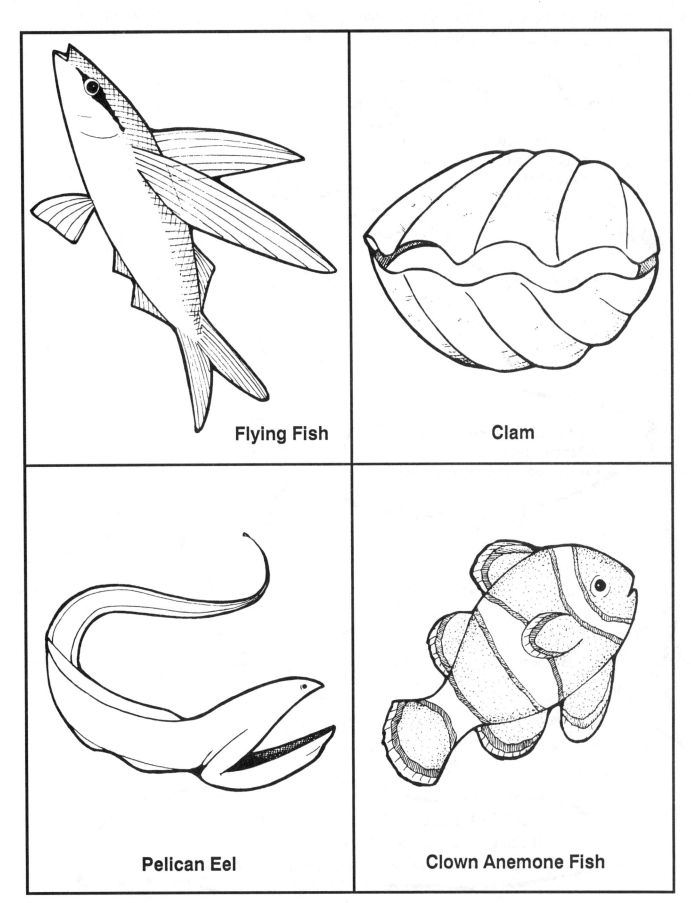

Flying Fish

Clam

Pelican Eel

Clown Anemone Fish

Believe It or Not!

Make a special spot on the blackboard or chart called "Believe It or Not!" Print or post a new fact in this spot each day. Read and discuss each amazing fact with your class.

The **ANGLER FISH** goes fishing.
A fishing rod hangs from its head.
It even has bait.
There is a "light" at the end of
the rod.

The **STARFISH** can grow a new arm.

It can even grow a new body.

The **FLYING FISH** leaps out of the water then flies! He can't fly far, but he can fly fast—about 30 miles an hour.

The **SEA ANEMONE** eats fish.

But it protects the clown fish.

And the clown fish brings it food!

The **TUNA** travels a lot.
By the time it is 15 years old, it will have gone 1 million miles (1.6 million kilometers)!

The **ELECTRIC EEL** really is electric.
It can give an electric shock.
It can make enough electricity to light up a Christmas tree!

38

Ocean Chants

Writing an Ocean Chant

1. Duplicate the ocean chant below onto chart paper, an overhead projector, or the chalkboard for all the students to see.

2. Model the chant for students; then repeat the words together.

Ocean Chant

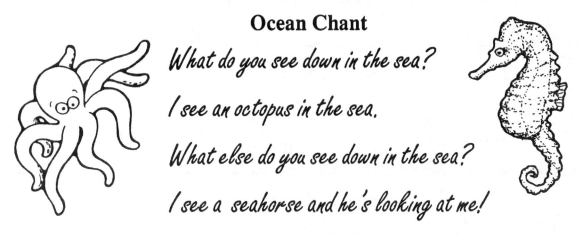

What do you see down in the sea?

I see an octopus in the sea.

What else do you see down in the sea?

I see a seahorse and he's looking at me!

3. Brainstorm a list of sea animals with the class. Create a web or word bank of ocean creatures. Use chart paper, an overhead projector, or the chalkboard so everyone can view the words. It may be helpful to put a picture next to each word so the students will remember what the word is.

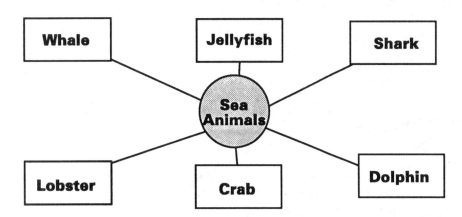

4. Make a large chart of the worksheet on page 40. With the whole group, model filling in the blanks with words from the word bank.

5. Have each student choose a partner. Direct them to create their own chants. They may use words from the word bank or they may brainstorm other words. Have students illustrate their chants in the space provided.

6. After the pairs have written their chants, have them form small groups in which they can share their writing.

Ocean Chants *(cont.)*

With a partner, write an ocean chant. Draw a picture in the box below.

Written by: _____

Illustrated by: _____

What do you see down in the sea?

I see a(n) _____ **in the sea.**

What else do you see down in the sea?

I see a (n) _____

and he's looking at me!

40

Fishy Games to Play

Use the cards on pages 42-43 for these games. If additional cards are desired, the concentration cards on pages 36-37 may be used.

Guess What It Is!

This is a guessing game for two people. Have students choose a partner and look at and read the sea animal cards together. Have them cut out the cards and put them in a box and mix them up.

To Play—Have students take out a sea animal card without telling the partner what it is. The partner may ask five yes or no questions. Then he or she must guess what the card says. Then partners switch roles.

Who Am I?

This is a guessing game for 10 to 20 people. Make extra copies of the sea animal card. Divide the class into two teams. Each child from Team A takes a card from the box. He or she must keep it a secret. Pin or tape it on the back of a person from Team B. When everyone in Team B has a card on his or her back, the game begins.

To Play—Everyone on Team B circulates about, asking yes or no questions. When 3 minutes are up, everyone sits down. Then each child guesses what he or she is. Now the teams change places.

Fish Cards

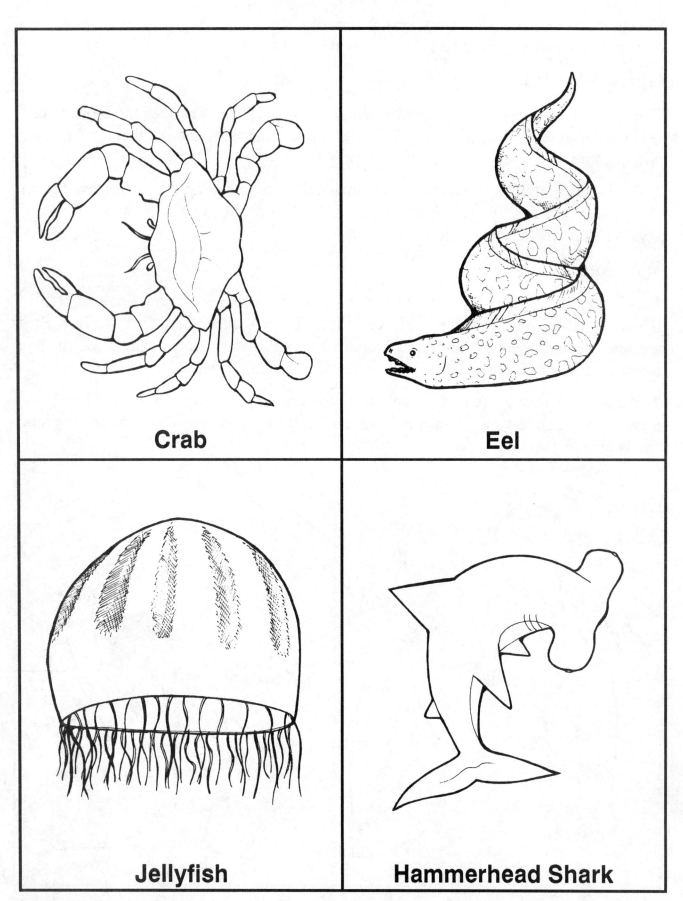

Crab

Eel

Jellyfish

Hammerhead Shark

Fish Cards *(cont.)*

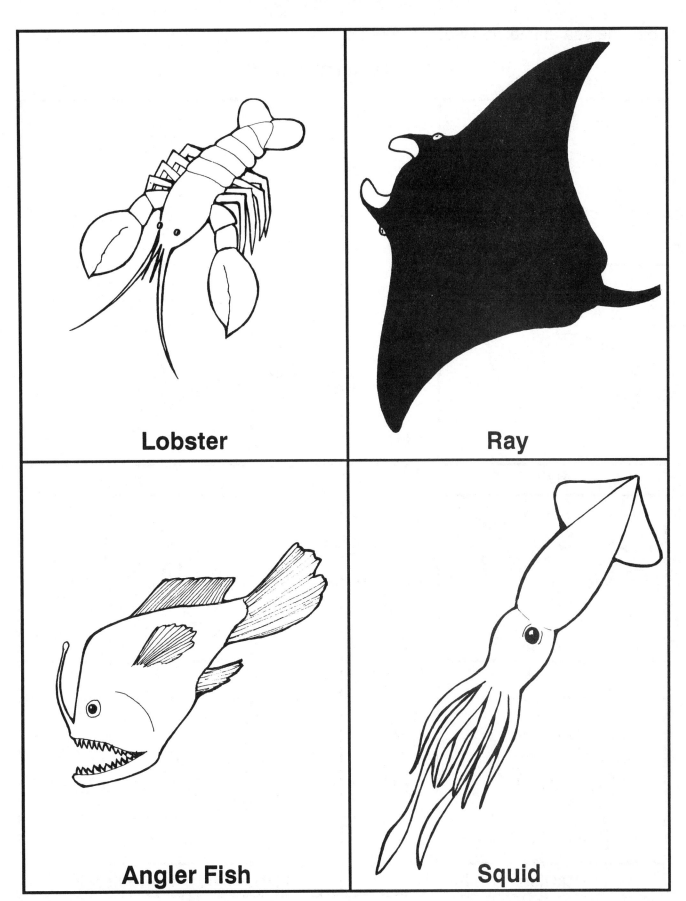

Lobster

Ray

Angler Fish

Squid

Would You Rather . . .

Color the sea animal you would rather be.

Would you rather be a:

dolphin

or a

seahorse

fish

or an

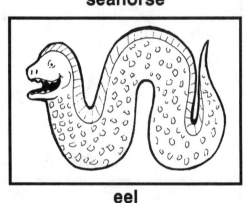

eel

whale

or an

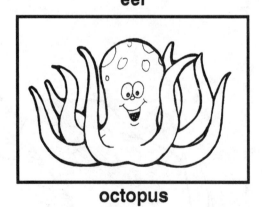

octopus

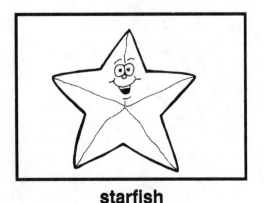

starfish

or a

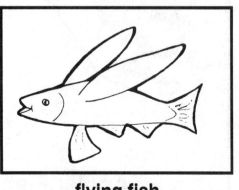

flying fish

Name_____

Dave the Octopus

Color pages 45 and 46. Cut out the legs. Count the number of dots on each leg and paste the leg to the matching number on the octopus.

Name _____

Dave the Octopus (cont.)

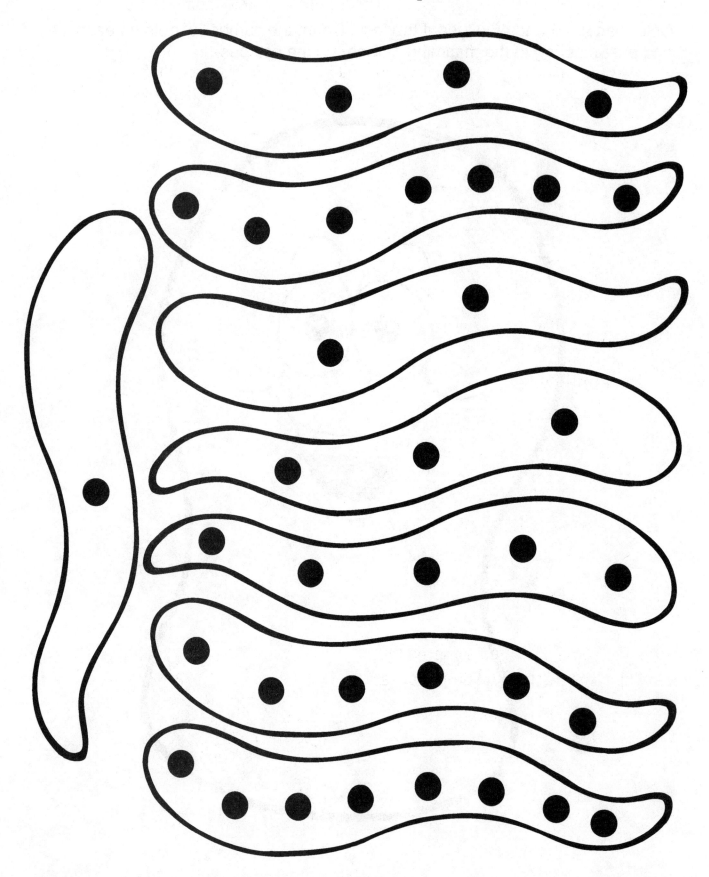

Draw a Story

Tell this story to the children. Illustrate it a bit at a time on the chalkboard, as shown below. You may wish to simplify or expand on the story. Children love to hear this type of story over again. After the children are familiar with the story, provide them with chalkboards or paper and crayons and let them draw and tell the story. Share *More Tell and Draw Stories* and *Lots More Tell and Draw Stories* by Margaret Jean Oldfield.

Sea Thing

Once there was a sea thing.
Who lived in a dark cave, under a rock.
All you could see were his two round eyes.
He hid in there, afraid of the sea.

One day two eels swam by.
He shut his eyes.
And sat very still.

When all was quiet,
He peeked out.
He saw 24 bubbles floating up!

"It's a sea monster!" he cried.
He shrivelled further into his cave,
Staring out—
Filled with fear.

But only some seaweed slithered by.
Catching the bubbles on their leaves.

by D. Williams

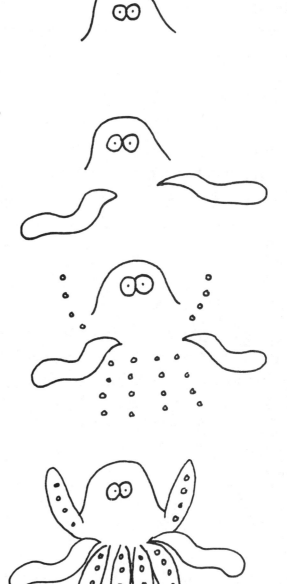

Living Graphs

Do this as a group activity so that all the children participate in making and then interpreting the graph.

"What Is Your Favorite Sea Animal?" Graph

Preparation: Make a graph on chart paper as shown in the diagram below. Copy several pictures of the sea animal cards on pages 42-43. Make the columns in the graph wide enough to fit the pictures.

Making the Graph:
Work with a small group of children at a time. Ask each child to tell you his/her favorite sea animal from the choices available and to choose it from the pile. Print or have the children print their names on their choices. Then help each child paste the card in the correct place on the graph. Add your own choice to the graph. When everyone has had a turn, call the children together to interpret the graph.

Interpreting the graph:
Ask several children to show where they pasted their squares.

Ask all the children who liked crabs best to clap their hands.

Ask all the children who liked eels best to stand up and turn around.

Ask all the children who liked jellyfish best to jump up and down. Count the children who liked jellyfish best. Then count the jellyfish cards on the graph. Compare and discuss. Do the same for each sea animal and think of a different movement for each animal.

Ask which sea animal is the most popular. How do they know?

Ask which sea animal is the least popular? How do they know?

Display the graph in the classroom.

WHAT IS YOUR FAVORITE SEA ANIMAL?		
		May
Mrs. Kay		Mike
Helena	Karen	Felipe
Rick	Marie	Joanna
CRAB	**EEL**	**JELLYFISH**

Other Graph Topics

Have you ever been to the ocean?

Can you swim?

Do you own any fish?

What is your favorite seafood?

Who Am I?

I am very cranky. I like to be alone.

If I am put in a tank with a lot of others, we will fight.

Connect the dots to find out.

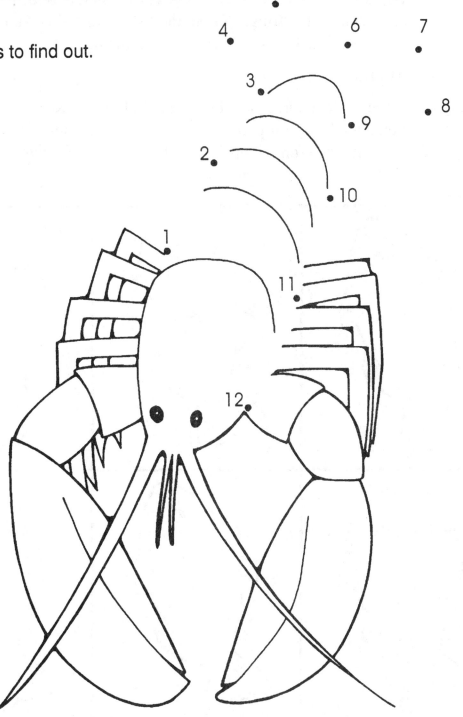

I am a _____

Going Fishing

Materials: pencils; string pieces; magnets; paper clips; bucket; scissors

Directions:

Cut a piece of string about 24 inches/60 cm long. Tie a pencil to one end of the string. Tie a magnet to the other end of the string. Cut out the fish cards below and on page 51. Clip a paper clip onto the top of each card. Put the cards in the bucket.

How to Play the Game:

Go fishing with a friend. Take turns catching a fish. Pull it out. Read the number on the fish. Count up to that number. Your partner will see if you are right. If you are right, you can keep the fish. If you are wrong, plop the fish back into the bucket.

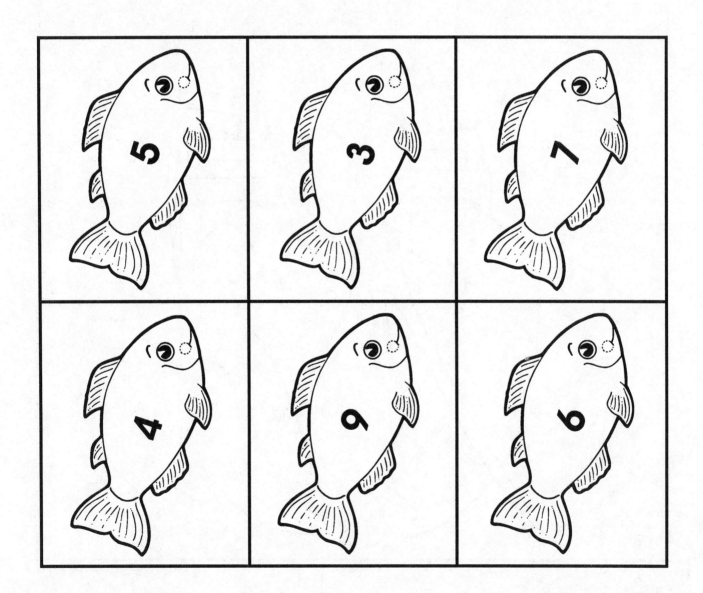

Going Fishing *(cont.)*

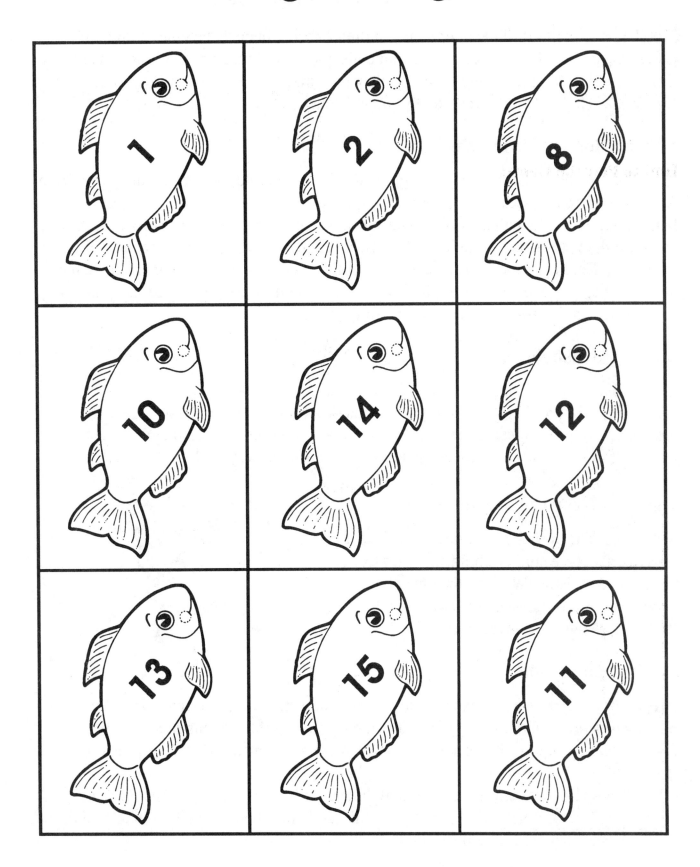

Fun With Seashells

Go on a field trip to the beach. Ask the children to bring buckets labelled with their names. Challenge the children to find and collect as many different shells as possible. Encourage the children to study their shells with a magnifying glass. If you do not live near the beach you may be able to buy some seashells to complete the activities.

Display the Seashell Collection

Materials: piece of cardboard or an egg carton for each child; felt pens; glue or masking tape; magnifying glasses
Directions: Have the children label their pieces of cardboard or egg cartons with their names. Ask them to choose their six best shells. Have them glue or tape each shell to the cardboard. Challenge them to search in the shell books to discover the name of each of their six shells. Ask them to print the name of each shell on the cardboard. Display the collections. Invite other classes to come and see them.

Sort the Seashells

Materials: variety of shells, 4 boxes, 2 trays, magnifying glasses
Directions: Have the children study the shells, using magnifying glasses. Have them sort the shells into groups, using the boxes or trays. Ask how they sorted them. Have them explain it to a friend. Ask students to sort them a different way.

Can You Hear the Seashells?

Materials: conch shells of various sizes
Directions: Have students hold shells up to their ears and listen. What do they hear? Have them ask friends what they hear and try to figure out why this happens.

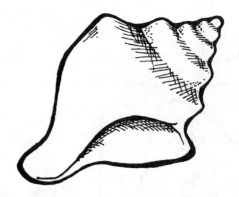

Study a Sand Dollar

Preparation: Obtain a few sand dollars from a shell store or the beach. Carefully crack one open to reveal the inside. Display them on a piece of black construction paper. Display photographs of live sand dollars. Read *Sand Dollar, Sand Dollar* by Joyce Audy dos Santos.
Directions: Have students study the sand dollars with a magnifying glass. Find the "poinsettia" star on the back. Find out what is inside the shell. Ask children to find the "little doves" that are inside the sand dollar.

Sea Simulations

Sharks

Sharks vary greatly in size. The largest kind of shark can grow to 60 feet (18 m) long, while the smallest sharks may measure only four inches (10 cm). To give students an idea of the sizes of some of these fish, tape a 14-foot (4 m) length of masking tape to the floor of the classroom to represent a nurse shark. Have students predict how many children lined up single file would equal that 14-foot length. Then have students line up on the chalk or masking tape. Was anyone able to make a correct prediction? Follow the same procedure but this time use a 20-foot (6 m) line to represent a thresher shark.

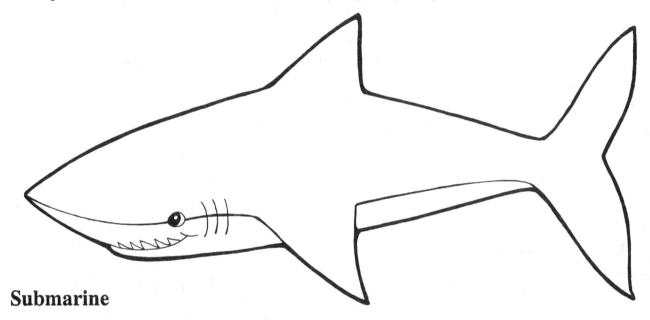

Submarine

Use an appliance box to create a mini-submarine. First cut an access hole in the back of the box. Next, paint the inside a dark blue or black. Cut out portholes for viewing and cover with plastic wrap or blue acetate. Draw pictures of marine plants and animals on the outside of the box. Hang fish in front of the windows. (Use pictures from magazines or enlarge the patterns from this book on pages 71-75.) Next, add tubes, lights, and gauges to the inside and outside of the box for an authentic look. Stock your submarine with books, pictures, shells, and other ocean wonders. You may even want to supply a flashlight so students can look out into the vast blue sea and imagine what it would be like to be inside a submarine.

Sea Water Experiments

Sea animals live in sea water. Demonstrate these experiments for your class so they can see how sea water is different from the fresh water lakes or ponds students may have near their homes.

Experiment 1

How do we know that ocean and sea water contain salt?

Materials: pie pan; 2 cups/480 mL ocean or sea water (You can make your own by mixing 2 tsp/10mL of salt with 2 cups/480mL of water.)

Directions:

Pour the water into a pan.

Place the pan in a warm, dry place.

Allow water to evaporate—this usually takes a few days.

Make observations.

Experiment 2

Why does an iceberg float?

Materials: a glass jar; water; a freezer; scale

Directions

Fill the jar to the top with water. Weigh and record the weight.

Carefully place the jar in the freezer.

Close the freezer door; in three hours, observe what has taken place.

Weigh the jar again and compare this weight with its pre-frozen weight.

Experiment 3

Is it easier to float in the ocean or in fresh water?

Materials: 1 egg; 1 jar filled with fresh water; 1 jar filled with ocean water (You can make your own by mixing 2 tsp/10 mL of salt with 2 cups/480 mL of water.)

Directions

Put the egg in the jar of fresh water.

Observe what happens.

Put the egg in the jar of ocean water.

Observe what happens.

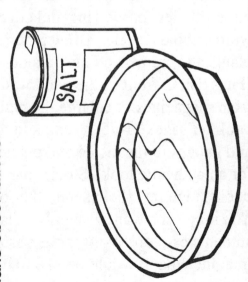
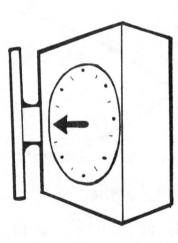
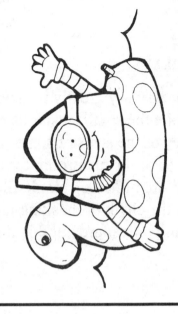

54

Dancing Fish

Try this simple experiment. Children will watch in amazement as the fish dance to the top of the container.

Materials: large glass container; raisins; baking soda; vinegar

Directions:

1. Fill a glass container with water. Mix in ⅓ cup (83 mL) of vinegar and 2 teaspoons (10 mL) of baking soda. Stir gently to avoid the mixture spilling over.

2. Add a few raisins to represent fish into the container. They will sink to the bottom at first, but then they will rise to the surface. The "fish" will continue rising to the surface and sinking back to the bottom for several hours.

Why it works: When the vinegar and baking soda are combined, they create a chemical reaction which produces carbon dioxide. The carbon dioxide bubbles collect on the raisins on the bottom of the jar. Since the bubbles are lighter than the water, they lift the raisins to the surface where several of the bubbles escape into the air. The raisins once again sink to the bottom where they collect more bubbles, and the process continues.

Silly Sea Songs

Sing these silly sea songs. Make up some more verses. Have fun drawing pictures about the songs.

"Old Sea Sailor"

(To the tune of "Old McDonald")
Old Sea Sailor went to sea,
Eeee Iiii Eeee Iiii Oooo,
And in this sea he saw a humpback,
Eeee Iiii Eeee Iiii Oooo,
With a la la here,
And a la la there.
Here a la, there a la,
Everywhere a la la,
Old Sea Sailor went to sea,
Eeee Iiii Eeee Iiii Oooo.

And in this sea he saw a seal,
Eeee Iiii Eeee Iiii Oooo,
With a bark bark here,
And a bark bark there,
Here a bark, there a bark,
Everywhere a bark bark,
Old Sea Sailor went to sea,
Eeee Iiii Eeee Iiii Oooo.

And in this sea he saw a fish,
Eeee Iiii Eeee Iiii Oooo,
With a bubble bubble here,
And a bubble bubble there,
Here a bubble, there a bubble,
Everywhere a bubble bubble,
Old Sea Sailor went to sea,
Eeee Iiii Eeee Iiii Oooo.

"Take Me Out to the Ocean"

(To the tune of "Take Me Out to the Ballgame")
Take me out to the ocean
Take me out to the sea
There goes a starfish and sand dollar,
I'm having such fun, I've just got to holler
Oh, it's swim, swim, swim, underwater
Catch a ride on a whale, don't fear,
For the sea animals are our friends,
Let's give a great big cheer!

56

Art Activities

Choose the art activities that are appropriate for your students.

Fun on a Stick

Materials: paper, lightweight cards, felt pens, scissors, glue, tape, popsicle sticks

Directions: Let children draw a sea creature and color it in bright colors. Then glue the picture onto lightweight cards and cut it out. Tape a craft stick to the back to make a handle. Let children try the following activities:

- Find a friend and play with their sea creatures together.
- Make up a puppet play with a friend, using the sea creatures.

- Pretend the sandbox is the bottom of the ocean. Make a home for their sea creature by adding plants or rocks to the sandbox. Stick the creature into the sand.
- Share sea creatures with the class. Make them talk. Ask them to tell the class all about themselves—what they eat, where they live; what they are.

Fish Prints

Materials: several fresh fish of different shapes and sizes, paper towels, powder paint, white paper

Teacher Preparation: Buy fresh fish with large scales. Offer one color per fish. Include a small squid! This activity will show the children the texture and body parts of a fish.

Directions: Dry the fish with the paper towel. Paint the fish with one color, covering all of one side of the fish. Carefully place a sheet of white paper onto the fish. Press gently with a flat, dry hand. Lift the paper off and allow to dry.

Paper Plate Aquarium

Materials: paper plates; scissors; paste; stapler; felt pens; plastic wrap; sand; pebbles; scraps of yarn, sponge, tissue, etc.

Teacher Preparation: Cut out the center of paper plate, leaving the narrow rim — one for each child. Each child will need one rim, the center piece, and one other paper plate.

Directions: Children will color the center of the paper plate the color of water. Draw sea creatures onto the cut out center section of the other paper plate. Cut out. Paste the sea creatures, sand, pebbles, scraps of wool, sponge, tissue onto the plate. Take the rim and staple it upside down onto the first plate to make a frame. Stretch plastic wrap across the opening of your aquarium. Staple, glue, or tape it so it stays.

Art Activities *(cont.)*

Shell Collage

Materials: pieces of various shells; pieces of wood or driftwood; scallop and clam shells from food store; strong glue

Directions: Clean the wood to ensure the shells will adhere. Choose pieces of shells and experiment by placing them on the piece of wood. Make a design or a picture with the shells. Apply glue all over one side of the wood. Apply glue to the back of each shell and press onto the wood. Allow to dry undisturbed. Print initials with permanent felt pen on back of wood.

Mobiles

Materials: coat hangers; neon felt pens; blue crepe paper strips; scissors; drawing paper; thread or string; tape; patterns on pages 71-75

Directions: Let children draw and color fish of different shapes and sizes. Cut them out. Tape a piece of string or thread to the back of each fish. Tie the fish to the coat hanger, varying the lengths of string. Tape crepe paper pieces to the hanger to be the water. Hang up the coat hanger.

Water Jars

Materials: baby food jars with lids; pieces of brightly colored cellophane; adhesive or masking tape; permanent fine point felt pens; clear or white plastic lids; scissors; foam trays

Directions: Have children draw tiny fish on the plastic or foam with the permanent felt pens. Cut them out. Cut out pieces of cellophane in the shape of plants or fish. Ask children to choose their favorites and put them in the jar. Fill the jar with water. Screw the lid on very tightly. Tape it on with adhesive or masking tape. Make the fish swim by shaking the water jar gently.

Art Activities *(cont.)*

Wax Crayon Melts

Materials: wax crayon bits; wax paper; old iron; newspaper; sparkles; muffin trays

Teacher Preparation: Spread the newspaper over the tables. Chop or shred the crayons into tiny bits, using a grater or sharp knife. Put the crayon bits into muffin trays, sorted by color. Cut the wax paper into pieces about 12 inches (30 cm) long. Fold in half.

Directions: Have children open the wax paper and sprinkle crayon bits onto the bottom piece. Sprinkle on sparkles. Close the wax paper carefully. Put a piece of newspaper on top and iron with a warm iron. Draw a fish shape onto the wax paper. Cut out. Mount on the window with clear tape. Or, tape a piece of string to the fish and hang him from the window frame so he can flutter in the breeze.

Stained Glass Fish

Materials: wax paper; liquid starch in bowls; paintbrushes; paste; crayons; tissue paper; construction paper; scissors

Teacher Preparation: Cut tissue paper into small pieces about 2" to 5" (5 cm x 13 cm). Cut 9" x 12" (23 cm x 30 cm) pieces of wax paper. Put out the materials.

Directions: Children can draw a fish shape on the wax paper with a wax crayon. Have them make it as big as they can. Cut out the wax paper fish. Paint the fish with liquid starch. Place bits of rainbow tissue paper all over the fish. Overlap some! Let the fish dry. Make eyes or a mouth out of construction paper. Paste onto the fish. Hang or tape onto the window so the sun can shine through!

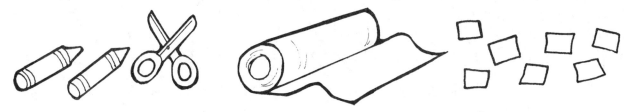

Art Activities (cont.)

Fishbowls without Water

Materials: wide mouthed glass jars (honey, jam jar, etc); shell and rock pieces; sand; paper; paste; scissors; felt pens; neon paper scraps

Directions: Draw and color various fish and sea creatures. Decorate with neon paper bits. Cut out. Paste onto the inside of the jars. Put the sand, rocks, shells inside the jar.

Swimming Masks

Materials: cardboard or stiff construction paper; scissors; plastic wrap; string; tape; pattern (page 63)

Directions: Draw a mask onto the cardboard, using the pattern. Cut it out. Carefully cut out the center space. Cut a piece of plastic wrap to fit the mask. Tape it onto one side of the mask. Poke a hole on each side of the mask. Thread 8-inch (20 cm) piece of string through each hole. Tie the mask on and dive in!

Sea Murals

Materials: large sheets of mural paper; newspapers; paints; scissors; water jars; felt pens; paintbrushes; glue; paper

Preparation: This is best done outside by clipping or taping a long piece of paper to a fence. An end roll of heavyweight paper is often available from newspaper publishers. Set out the supplies. Divide the class into groups of 4 to 6 people.

Note: The murals can be used as backdrop scenery for creative drama.

Directions: Have children paint the ocean background onto the mural paper. Try the wet brush technique by using a very wet brush. Paint the sand, rocks, sea plants, coral, and various colors of the water. While this is drying, draw and color tropical fish of many colors and designs. Cut them out. Decide cooperatively where to paste them on. Draw and color other sea creatures, cut them out, and paste them on.

60

The Sea Turtle

Study the pictures below.

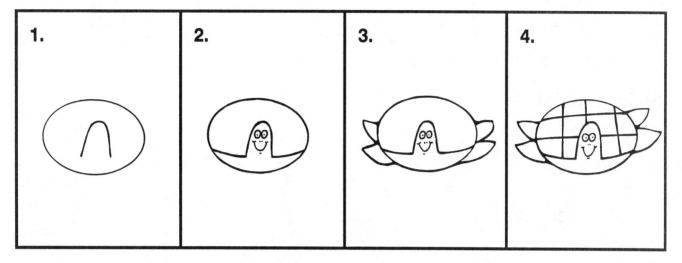

Now draw your own.

Fishy Necklace

1. Decorate the fish.

2. Cut them out.

3. Punch 2 holes in each fish.

4. String them together with yarn.

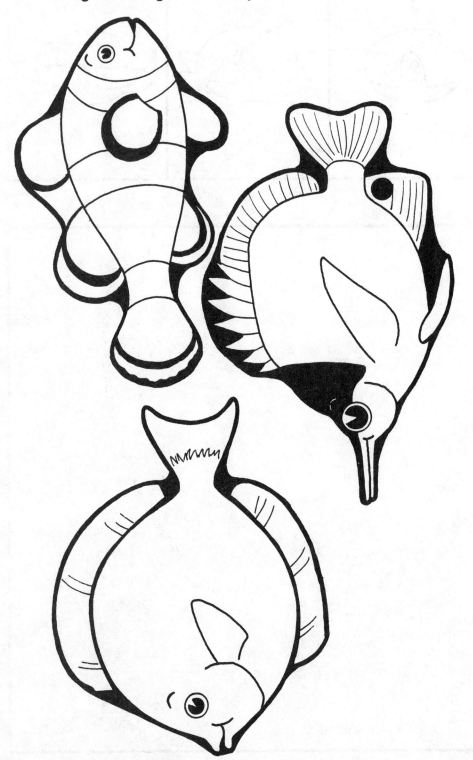
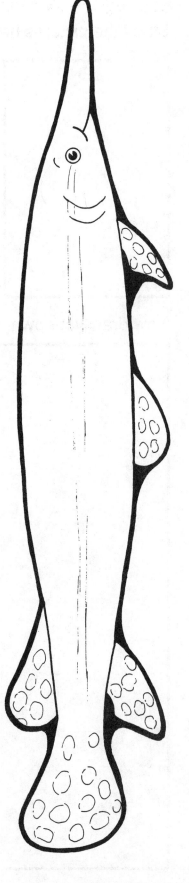

62

Swimming Mask

See page 60 for directions.

Art

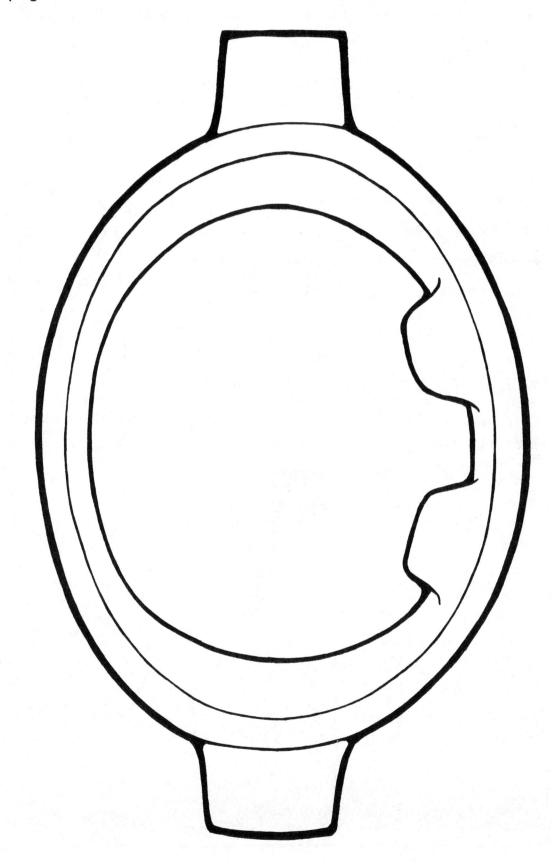

Let's Cook

These general directions will help you get ready for any cooking project. Cooking with children is an ambitious activity during which you must be at the controls. The children are involved in measuring, mixing, smelling, and eating.

Teacher Preparation:

- Arrange for a helper to come (a parent or other adult volunteer).

- Post the rules (page 65).

- Print the recipe on a chart.

- Read the rules to the class and discuss.

- Organize at least two small groups.

- Spread out newspaper or plastic tablecloth.

- Put out all the equipment and ingredients.

Directions:

1. Put the recipe chart where it is easily seen.

2. Ensure that the other children are busy and supervised.

3. Take the cooking group to a table. Play "Guess what it is!" Have children close eyes and smell each ingredient.

4. Read the recipe to your group a bit at a time.

5. Give each child a turn to add an ingredient or stir.

6. Cook or bake.

7. Have a Tasting Party!

64

1. Wash your hands.

2. Wear an apron or cover-up.

3. Ask a grownup to help.

4. Take turns.

5. Measure carefully.

6. Help clean up.

Baking and Cooking Rules

Seafaring Recipes

Seafood is nutritious. Fish contains protein which is needed to build and repair body cells. Some fish, such as tuna, also provide vitamin D, which helps the body absorb calcium and phosphorous for healthy bones and teeth. In addition, fish have niacin which works with other B vitamins to use energy in human cells.

Try these delicious seafaring treats for a healthful addition to the students' diet.

Tuna in a Cone

Make tuna salad. (Use only dolphin-safe tuna, please.) Then fill an ice cream cone with the mixture. Top with an olive half or a cherry tomato.

Ingredients: One 6½ or 7 ounce (about 200g) can of tuna; ⅓ cup (about 100 mL) mayonnaise; 2 tablespoons (30 mL) sweet pickle relish; ¼ teaspoon (1 mL) salt, if desired

Directions:

- Drain the tuna; place into a mixing bowl.
- Break the tuna into chunks, using a fork.
- Add the mayonnaise, pickle relish, and salt; stir with a fork.
- Scoop the mixture into ice cream cones; add an olive or cherry tomato to the top.

Imitation Fish

This may not qualify for the most nutritious treat, but it is an eye-catcher! Make lime or blueberry gelatin in a new, unused fish bowl. Then fill it with gummy candy fish. Once the gelatin sets, the bowl will resemble a mini-aquarium.

Seafaring Recipes *(cont.)*

Make a Salmon Sandwich

Ingredients:

large tin of salmon

jar of mayonnaise

4 sticks of celery

pepper

brown bread

margarine

Equipment:

bowl

can opener

big spoon

knife

cutting board

measuring cup

serving plate

Directions:

Open the can of salmon. Drain it. Put the salmon into the bowl. Measure $1/3$ cup (about 100 mL) mayonnaise into the bowl. Mix. Wash the celery. Cut into small pieces. Mix into the salmon mixture. Add a dash of pepper. Spread the margarine onto the bread. Spread the salmon mixture onto the bottom slices of bread. Put on the top slices of bread. Cut each sandwich into four pieces. Put them on the plate and serve.

Sea Star Sandwiches

Make sandwiches using your favorite salmon spread (see above), fish cakes, or sardines. Add cheese, lettuce, etc. With a star shaped cookie cutter, press out a star shape. Decorate your sea star sandwich with cream cheese and olive eyes.

Sea Animal Games

Octopus

Materials: playing field; sponge ball

Directions:

Mark the playing field with a goal line at each end. Choose one child to be the octopus; the rest of the class are fish. The object of the game is for the octopus to catch the fish by tagging or hitting them with the sponge ball. If a fish is hit or tagged, he or she becomes frozen in place and is now an octopus tentacle. The tentacles may help the octopus by using their outstretched hands to tag fish. Only the octopus may move around; the tentacles must stay in the same spot where they were caught.

To begin play, all the fish line up at one goal line. The octopus calls out, "Fish, fish, swim in my ocean." At this command, the fish must "swim" (hop, walk, run, or any movement agreed upon before the game) across the ocean to the opposite goal. Play continues until all but one fish has been caught. The last fish is the winner.

Crab Races

Directions:

Have children practice walking like crabs. (See illustration.) Once they are able to move in that position, they are ready to race. The children may have individual or team races. Children may race forward or backward.

Extension: Crab soccer can be played by dividing the children into two teams. The object is for a team to kick a ball into the other team's goal.

Make a Life-Sized Baby Whale

Make a life-sized baby humpback whale as a class project! (Make two if you wish—one male, one female.) Research to find out all about him. Make him a good home, and give it a name. Make a book about the baby whale. Have an Open House for family or other classes to share all of this.

Our Baby Whale

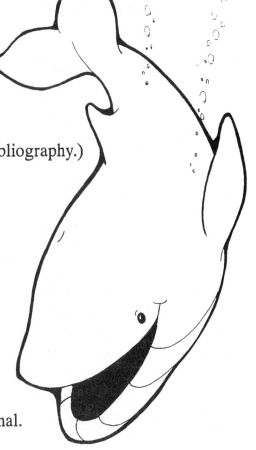

1. **How big is a baby humpback whale?**
   Estimate; find out.
   Measure onto a roll of paper using a tape measure.
   Cut the paper to the correct length.

2. **What does a baby humpback whale look like?**
   Find pictures of humpbacks—study and discuss. (See bibliography.)
   Note the shape, body parts, and colors.
   Draw the outline on the paper with pencil, then marker.
   Draw the various parts and markings.
   Help the children paint it.
   Use felt pen to outline and define. Cut it out.

3. **How fat is a baby humpback whale?**
   Trace the whale's outline onto another piece of paper.
   This other side could also be painted if desired.
   Staple the two sides together, leaving openings.
   Find out how fat a baby humpback is.
   Stuff in scrunched newspaper to make it three-dimensional.
   Staple shut.

4. **Where does it live?**
   This is a good time to discuss/debate whether a whale should be kept in captivity.
   The ideas could be recorded on a chart—"Should a Whale be Kept in an Aquarium?"
   Discuss "What Does an Orca Need?" and make a list.
   Paint a large mural of an ocean, or use the previous murals.
   Mount this on a wall.
   Hang or staple the whale onto the ocean mural.

5. **What does it eat?**
   Find out what it eats.
   Make food for it to find, using felt pens or crayons on paper, then cutting it out.
   Paste these onto the mural.

Make a Life-Sized Baby Whale (cont.)

6. **Give it a name.**

   Make a list of suggestions; then choose the best by voting.

7. **What is his family like?**

   Find out all about its family life by reading books, studying photographs, etc.

   Draw or paint its family. Cut out and paste on the mural.

8. **What does it like to do?**

   Find out what humpbacks like to do and who their friends are.

   Draw or paint their friends. Cut out and paste them onto the mural.

9. **How can we keep it safe?**

   Find out who its enemies are.

   Draw and cut out whaling ships. Mount them in a corner of the mural—far away.

   Tape string to the bows and tie them to a wharf.

   Make boats and ships.

   Paste them on the top of the "ocean" to guard over the baby whale, or mount them near the whaling ships to make them stay away.

   Make oil tankers and mount them far away or in dry dock.

10. **Do some creative writing.**

    Write a class-dictated story about your friend—fiction or nonfiction. Title it "The Baby Whale." Make it into a book.

11. **Hold an Open House**

    Invite the students' families or another class to come and meet your friend, the baby whale. See page 78 for invitations.

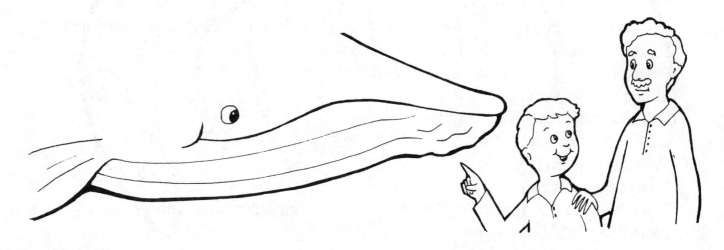

Sea Animal Patterns

Sea Animal Patterns *(cont.)*

Sea Animal Patterns *(cont.)*

Sea Animal Patterns *(cont.)*

74

Sea Animal Patterns *(cont.)*

Bulletin Board

Wall Collage

You can turn an entire wall into an ocean scene using student artwork projects.

1. Staple or tape the sea murals onto the wall. (See page 60.)
2. Staple or tape blue construction paper or crepe paper around the murals.
3. Cut a long piece of brown paper to fit the length of the wall. Cut it in half lengthwise in a rolling fashion to simulate the sandy bottom of the sea. Staple or tape this on the wall close to the floor.
4. Staple or tape some of the "stuffed sea creatures" onto the wall. (See page 26).
5. Twist long pieces of crepe paper into seaweed shapes and staple on.
6. Select some of the fish from fish prints, sponge painting, and neon fish and staple on.
7. Set some of the shell collages out along the floor on the "sand" base.
8. Tie a string across in front of the wall collage about a foot from the wall. Hang up some of the coat hanger mobiles.
9. Use this wall collage as a background for Creative Drama activities.

An Open House

When using a whole language thematic approach, it is important to get the full support of the parents. They need to see that learning this way is challenging, productive, fun, and successful. One way to share the children's accomplishments is to have an Open House. Plan to have the Open House after you have completed the unit. The easiest time is during the school day. The more ambitious time is in the evening. This increases the chance that all children will be able to "perform" for their families.

Plan. Explain to the children what an Open House is. Tell them it is a fun way to share school with their families. Explain it is a chance to show all they have learned. Discuss what they could share.

Prepare. Give the children time to prepare and to finish their projects. If they would like to share a song, puppet play, or play, help them to practice. Send out the invitations. Tidy the activity centers. Encourage the children to teach their families how to do the activities. Display the children's work attractively. Plan the seating. Ask the children how many guests they are bringing. Have a dress rehearsal. Share the "presentation" with another class. Practice showing imaginary families around the room. Ask the children to find the things they would like to show their families. Ask them to plan how they will teach their families at the activity centers.

Have Fun! Remember it is the process, not the product, that counts now. Families have few opportunities to see their children "perform," so they will appreciate your efforts, and they will enjoy the Open House! Remember to use the Open House as an opportunity to reinforce self-esteem—both yours and the children's.

Suggestions for Open House Preparations

Meet your guests at the door and give them masks and imaginary air tanks! Warn them that they are diving deep into the sea! Sing a "Silly Sea Song." Share all the art projects. Share your favorite sea animal book. Share the activity on page 44 with guests and ask them what they would rather be. Teach each family how to do the activity center activities, visual memory games, and puzzles. Serve them the students' cooking!

Letters to Parents

We Are Going on a Trip!

We are visiting the _____.

We will travel by _____.

It will cost _____.

Children are asked to bring _____

_____.

Thank you,

_____

Come Jump in the Ocean with Us!

We have just finished studying Sea Animals. We would like to share our discoveries with you.

Place: _____

Date: _____

Time: _____

Bibliography

Nonfiction Books

Cousteau, Jacques Yves. *The Ocean World of Jacques Cousteau*. Danbury Press, 1974.

Crow, Sandra Lee. *The Wonderful World of Seals and Whales*. National Geography Society, 1984.

Gibbons, Gail. *Whales*. Holiday House, 1992.

Jacobs, Francine. *Coral*. G.P. Putnam's Sons, 1980.

Malnig, Anita. *Where the Waves Break*. Carolrhoda, 1985.

Milton, Joyce. *Whales the Gentle Giants*. Random House, 1989.

Morris, Robert A. *Dolphin*. Harper & Row, 1975.

Morris, Robert A. *Seahorse*. Harper & Row, 1972.

Patent, Dorothy Hinshaw. *Humpback Whales*. Holiday House, 1989.

Phleger, Fred. *Red Tag Comes Back*. Harper & Row, 1961.

Podendorf, Illa. *Animals of Sea and Shore*. Children's, 1982.

Selsam, Millicent E. & Joyce Hunt. *A First Look At Whales*. Walker & Company, 1980.

Selsam, Millicent E. *Sea Monsters of Long Ago*. Four Winds Press, 1977.

Shaw, Evelyn. *Octopus*. Harper & Row, 1971.

Shawver, Mark. *Nature's Children: Whales*. Grolier Ltd, 1986.

Simon, Seymour. *Whales*. Thomas Y. Crowell, 1989.

Whittell, Giles. *The Story of 3 Whales*. World Wildlife Fund, Children's Books, 1988.

Wox, Wendy. *A Calico Book*. Contemporary Books, 1989.

Young, Jim. *When the Whale Came to My Town*. Alfred A. Knopf, 1974.

Fiction Books

Allen, Pamila. *Who Sank the Boat?* Coward-McCann, 1982.

Aruego, Jose. *Pilyo the Piranha*. Macmillan, 1971.

Barber-Starkey, Joe. *Jason & the Sea Otter*. Harbour, 1989.

Bowden, Joan Chase. *Why The Tides Ebb & Flow*. Houghton Mifflin, 1979.

Carle, Eric. *A House For Hermit Crab*. Picture Book Studio, 1987.

Cooke, Tom. *Grover's Adventure Under the Sea*. Random House, 1989.

Domanska, Janina. *I Saw a Ship A-Sailing*. Macmillan, 1972.

Dos Santos, Joyce Audy. *Sand Dollar, Sand Dollar*. J.B. Lippincott, 1980.

Dr. Seuss. *McElligot's Pool*. Random House, 1975.

Gomi, Taro. *Where's the Fish?* William Morrow, 1977.

Hoff, Syd. *Walpole*. Harper & Row, 1977.

Hughes, Shirley. *Lucy & Tom at the Seaside*. Victor Gollancz Ltd., 1987.

James, Simon. *My Friend Whale*. Bantam, 1991.

Johnston, Tony. *Whale Song*. G.P. Putnam's Sons, 1987.

Bibliography *(cont.)*

Kassian, Olena. *Flip the Dolphin Saves the Day.* Golden Press Book, 1984.

Kassler, Deirdre. *Lobster in My Pocket.* Ragweed Press, 1987.

Lionni, Leo. *Swimmy.* Pantheon, 1968.

McDonald, Megan. *Is This a House for Hermit Crab?* Orchard Books, 1990.

Oldfield, Margaret Jean. *Lots More Tell and Draw Stories.* Creative Storytime Press, 1973.

Oldfield, Margaret Jean. *More Tell and Draw Stories.* Creative Storytime Press, 1969.

Peet, Bill. *Cyrus the Unsinkable Sea Serpent.* Houghton Mifflin, 1975.

Peet, Bill. *Kermit The Hermit.* Houghton Mifflin, 1980.

Raffi. *Down by the Bay: Raffi Songs to Read.* Crown Publishers, 1987.

Rockwell, Anne. *At the Beach.* Macmillan, 1987.

Rosen, Michael & Quentin Blake. *Smelly Jelly Smelly Fish.* Walker Books, Ltd., 1986.

Rylant, Cynthia. *Henry & Mudge & the Forever Sea.* Bradbury Press, 1989.

Sargent, Susan & Donna Aaron Wirt. *My Favorite Place.* Abingdon, Press, 1983.

Steig, William. *Amos & Boris.* Farrar, Straus & Giroux, 1971.

Stevenson, James. *Clams Can't Sing.* Greenwillow Books, 1980.

Urgerer, Tomi. *Emile.* Harper & Brothers, 1960.

Waber, Bernard. *I Was All Thumbs.* Houghton Mifflin, 1975.

The Walt Disney Company. *The Little Mermaid Pop-up Book.* 1990.

Wildsmith, Brian. *Fishes.* Oxford University Press, 1987.

Records and Tapes

Diamond, Charlotte. *Diamonds & Dragons.* Hug Bug Records. "Rubber Blubber Whale."

Penner, Fred. *A House for Me.* Troubadour Records Ltd. "Michael Row the Boat Ashore,"

"Jack Was Every Inch a Sailor," "There's a Hole in the Bottom of the Sea."

Raffi. *Baby Beluga.* Troubadour. "Baby Beluga," "Water Dance"

"Be Kind To Your Web-Footed Friends," "There's a Hole in the Bottom of the Sea," "Three Little Fishies."

"Song of the Humpback Whale." CRM Records, Del Mar, California 92014.

Walt Disney. *Silly Songs.* Disney Cassettes. "Why Down Here Beneath the Ocean,"

Filmstrips

Let's Find Out About the Ocean by David C. Knight—filmstrip available from American School Publishers, 1-800-843-8855.

Adventure in Marineland—set of six filmstrips available from American School Publishers 1-800-843-8855.